What Is Scientology?

An Introductory Guide to the Church of Scientology and the Fundamental Scientology Beliefs and Principles

by Steven Greene

Table of Contents

Introduction 1

Chapter 1: What Is Scientology? 7

Chapter 2: The Fundamental Beliefs and Principles 11

Chapter 3: Understanding Scientology and Its Practices 17

Chapter 4: Scientology as it Relates to Other Religions 25

Chapter 5: The Ceremonies of Scientology 31

Chapter 6: Controversies Involving Scientology 37

Chapter 7: Important Pointers on Scientology 41

Conclusion 47

Introduction

We all are aware that many famous celebrities, including Tom Cruise, John Travolta, Kelly Preston and Kirstie Alley, are known to be members of Scientology. What prompted these well-known personalities to follow Scientology? There must be something significant about this belief that has attracted these celebrities.

And what about you? What comes to mind when you hear the word "Scientology"? Most people assume that it's about science since the word contains "scient(ia)", Latin for knowledge, and a derivative of "logos," a Greek word meaning "study of". But it's more than that.

Because Scientology is not exactly a mainstream religion, there are conflicting impressions about it. In some cultures, Scientology is classified as religion, while others believe it to be a cult. Still, some groups see it as a commercial enterprise, while others claim it's a non-profit organization. This just proves that most people don't fully understand Scientology. However, the believers and followers of Scientology claim it to be a religion following the intent of the original founder.

This book was written for those who want to learn what the Church of Scientology represents, and the basic principles and beliefs of Scientology. I intend to help clarify any incorrect perceptions while revealing what Scientology is really all about. Continue reading to discover the reason behind this oft-misjudged practice once and for all.

© Copyright 2015 by Miaf LLC - All rights reserved.

This document is geared towards providing reliable information in regards to the topic and issue covered. The publication is sold with the idea that the publisher is not required to render accounting, officially permitted, or otherwise, qualified services. If advice is necessary, legal or professional, a practiced individual in the profession should be ordered.

- From a Declaration of Principles which was accepted and approved equally by a Committee of the American Bar Association and a Committee of Publishers and Associations.

In no way is it legal to reproduce, duplicate, or transmit any part of this document in either electronic means or in printed format. Recording of this publication is strictly prohibited and any storage of this document is not allowed unless with written permission from the publisher. All rights reserved.

The information provided herein is stated to be truthful and consistent, in that any liability, in terms of inattention or otherwise, by any usage or abuse of any policies, processes, or directions contained within is solely and completely the responsibility of the recipient reader. Under no circumstances will any legal responsibility or blame be held against the publisher for any reparation, damages, or monetary loss due to the information herein, either directly or indirectly.

Respective authors own all copyrights not held by the publisher.

The information herein is offered for informational purposes solely, and is universal as so. The presentation of the information is without contract or any type of guarantee assurance.

The trademarks that are used are without any consent, and the publication of the trademark is without permission or backing by the trademark owner. All trademarks and brands within this book are for clarifying purposes only and are the owned by the owners themselves, not affiliated with this document.

Chapter 1: What Is Scientology?

Scientology is defined as the process of understanding your physical self and your spiritual self as you relate to other people around you. It could be your family, friends, and your environment. It also allows you to understand your connection with the universe and with God.

Scientology was first introduced into the world in 1952 by L. Ron Hubbard who claims that it is a religion anchored on the principle that the soul lives forever. It maintains a hierarchy of leaders in its structure who are primarily responsible in sharing its teachings and doctrines.

Scientology is a set of principles, beliefs and practices that govern the way people exist in relation to their spirituality. It teaches life after death, reincarnation and human immortality. Scientology demonstrates that the spirit may depart the body but lives on forever in different forms. The spirit transfers from one body to the next—infinitely—through births and deaths.

Scientology is further defined as a group of practices in a religion that believes that a person's experiences in his past lives affect the present. Thus, the sufferings of a person in previous lives may result in illnesses of the mind and body in his current life. It is therefore important to overcome these negative experiences by training the mind and the body.

In a nutshell, Scientology is indeed, a religion that follows certain principles and beliefs. But unlike other religions, it doesn't force its members to believe in dogmas on the pretext of faith alone. It allows its members to experience their own spiritual enlightenment in life using the principles of Scientology.

Chapter 2: The Fundamental Beliefs and Principles

There are numerous sets of beliefs and principles anchored on religious doctrines and ideologies that tend to confuse people. With the many beliefs and schools of thoughts that go around, it is important to carefully evaluate each array of principles and philosophies to determine which most resonates with you before embracing one of them.

What are the beliefs and principles of Scientology?

There are several beliefs and principles of Scientology that can further help you understand and appreciate its teachings:

- **Man is immortal**

    Scientology teaches that human beings are immortal. This is based on the belief that the spirit (thetan or life or source of life) of man lives forever. When a person dies his spirit departs the physical body and takes another body through birth. The spirit of man lives on and on from one person to the next. It affirms that the spirit transcends time and physical boundaries.

It is stressed that Scientology's final goal is immortality or living infinitely. An individual passes through different stages of human life before it finally reaches the stage of infinity.

Scientologists also believe that man is born good and the kind of life he will lead will depend on his actions as he relates to himself, his family, other people and the universe, which is composed of his experiences that are carried on to the next life. The result of his deeds in the past determines his disposition in the present life. The ultimate goal is to regain purity of spirit. When a person has reached this stage, it is believed that he has re-claimed what originally belongs to him: his capabilities, his freedom and his immortality.

- **Man's life experiences transcend one life time**

Scientology embraces reincarnation. It espouses the doctrine that the past experiences of an individual affect his current life unless these are resolved through *"Dianetics"*, a technique of removing the effects of the bad experiences in the past lifetimes. "Auditing" as dubbed by Scientology is used to apply dianetics to an individual to achieve an avenue of a new beginning for a person.

Painful experiences in previous lives may cause disorders, physical and mental illnesses, a disturbed mind, and other sufferings to the current life of the individual.

- **Human beings possess boundless capabilities**

Since Scientology believes in man being god-like, he can do practically anything. He can do what-god-can-only-do things. When an individual has attained purity in spirit, he is considered a free man. He has crossed what Scientology refers to as "the bridge to total freedom". Total freedom is a stage in the life of a human being where he is spiritually free from the burdens of humanity.

If a normal human being can do much, a man that has the qualities of God can do much more because he believes that God has limitless capabilities that were given to man.

- **There are 8 Dynamics to Existence**

Scientologists believe that the dynamic (urge for survival) of a person can be acted upon by outside factors which can then lead to man's 8 Dynamics of Existence.

1. **First Dynamic** – The person strives for his own survival and survives on his own, where outside connections do not count.

2. **Second Dynamic** – This is where family comes in. A couple marries, has children and become responsible parents.

3. **Third Dynamic** – This includes groups outside the family such as, colleagues, friends, social networks and the community.

4. **Fourth Dynamic** – This includes the survival of an individual amidst other races and other creeds. This involves the whole human race.

5. **Fifth Dynamic** – This is where the individual survives among all the living things around him such as plants and animals.

6. **Sixth Dynamic** – This includes the survival of man amidst the physical universe of MEST (Matter, Energy, Space, and Time).

7. **Seventh Dynamic** – This involves the survival of a person in the spirit world. The spirit world is a different entity from the physical world.

8. **Eighth Dynamic** – This is the survival of man as a God-like entity. It means that man has now attained the Supreme-Being state.

In conclusion, Scientology beliefs and principles are based mostly on the premise that the human spirit is the center of the human being without which, there can be no man; that the human spirit is in truth what Scientology considers as the "life or the source of life"; that this spirit can be rehabilitated into its purest state—the god-like state. Its spiritual capabilities can be put back for it to be able to perform what it existed for.

Scientology believes that there is a world that is free, a condition where man can freely and peacefully live. A state where there is no chaos, no war, no crimes or criminals, free from insanity; a state where a person has risen from his spiritual self to embrace the broader, spiritual level of mankind.

Chapter 3: Understanding Scientology and Its Practices

The practices of Scientology all come from "Dianetics", the writings and videos of L. Ron Hubbard who copyrighted the materials for his Church of Scientology. He disclosed that the writings that Scientology has is comparable to math because the words have exact meanings. That was the reason why he created a dictionary specifically for Scientology. Through this way, the members will not misinterpret the word and commit wrong practices.

The details of such practices are found below:

Auditing

Auditing is a Scientology practice where "auditors" are tasked to ask questions from "preclear" (lost) individuals. The auditors listen to their answers and then record them. Afterwards, the auditors will help the person achieve a "State of Clear" (no more false information in the person's beliefs and ideas) based on the Dianetics. It's like several levels of counseling until the preclear attains god-like abilities.

As believed in Scientology, auditing brings back the god-like qualities of man that he has previously possessed and catapults him to a state that resembles a condition that is similar to where god is.

However, before auditors can perform their assigned tasks, they must be trained intensively in the process with the use of an E-meter. This E-meter is a device that helps individuals gauge themselves and stay true to themselves so that they can recover from their past mistakes.

For non-Scientologists, this can be perceived as a psychoanalysis process, where counseling sessions by counselors (auditors) take place. The counselor listens to the person's input and then helps clarify the person's misunderstandings to reform him into a new being. But Scientologists are very vocal in clarifying that this is not psychoanalysis. In fact, they don't endorse psychoanalysis.

Silent Birth

This practice has a literal meaning. It means that silence is observed during birth. Those who are attending to the mother must not shout frantically or talk loudly. Scientologists believe that frenzied talking or shouting during birth - even if it was meant to encourage the mother to push - can have a lasting negative effect on the child later on in life.

When the child hears similar frantic shouts, he may feel depressed or anxious without knowing why.

Silent birth does not prohibit Caesarian sections (CS) or pain relievers though, if the mother desires so. The person can choose whatever diagnostic procedure she wants but all of these must be done in silence. Of course, during emergency situations when words have to be spoken to communicate, it should be done sparingly and in hushed tones. The general idea is to maintain silence during the birthing process. There are cited examples of the effect of non-silent birthing through the Dianetics.

Gradual Learning

This occurs when Scientologists learn from their own experiences and gradual learning takes place. This is because one of the main purposes of Scientology is to recover the god-like properties of its members. This can take place through gradual learning that goes through several levels, and is a lifetime process. The process must occur in an orderly fashion; a person cannot proceed to the next level, unless he has passed the previous level.

Observation of Scientology Holidays

Scientologists celebrate various holidays which include the following:

- **March 13 - L. Ron. Hubbard's birthday**

He was born March 13, 1911. Hubbard's birthday is celebrated by Scientologists all over the world. They celebrate this day by extending their helping hands to disaster-ridden individuals, human rights victims, conducting anti-drug campaigns and by spreading Scientology to non-believers.

- **September (2nd Sunday) - Auditors' Day**

This is a celebration and acknowledgement of the achievements of the auditors. Auditors are highly-regarded in Scientology because of their pivotal role in the community. Invitations to become an auditor are open to all members of the congregation.

- **February 22 – Celebrity Day**

This is a day of celebration for celebrities in Scientology. Celebrity membership is continually increasing as more and more famous names are joining the church. It has been reported that international celebrities are starting to join the ranks of Scientologists in America.

- **May 9 – Dianetics' Anniversary**

It was on May 9, 1950 that L. Ron Hubbard released his book entitled: "Dianetics: The Modern Science of Mental Health". From then on, this book has served as one of the sources of teachings of Scientology.

- **June 6 – Maiden Voyage of Freewinds Anniversary**

This is the celebration of the Maiden Voyage of the Freewinds. Freewinds is the ship where advance levels of retreats are conducted to qualified auditors, parishioners and staffs. It's where the Flag Ship Service Organization (FSSO) resides. The FSSO ministers are responsible for training the group to get to the highest level of spirituality that they can attain.

- **June 18 – Academy Day**

This is the celebration of the Scientology teaching method named Study Tech. Study Tech was developed by Hubbard. Study Tech serves as the "quick way" to learn Scientology.

- **September 4 – Clear Day**

This celebrates the establishment of the Clearing Course on September 4, 1965. The Clearing Course helps members to become "clear" and achieve the next level of spirituality.

- **October 7 – International Association of Scientologists' (IAS) Day**

This is the day that the IAS has defended the principles and beliefs of the church from external attacks. "Freedom Medals" are also awarded to members who have helped the IAS achieve their goals, and who have been active in defending Scientology.

- **December 31 – New Year's Eve**

This day is recognized by Scientologists as a day to acknowledge the accomplishments of members during the past year. It's also commemorated as a day to review the past and learn from it, and a day to move forward—a new chapter in one's life.

It's important to note that Scientologists usually celebrate the holidays they practiced in their previous religions. There's no ban against members who want to celebrate other types of holidays.

Chapter 4: Scientology as it Relates to Other Religions

Scientology is not a Christian religion because they don't believe that Jesus is the Savior and God. If you analyze its principles and beliefs, it's actually a smorgasbord of various religions such as Hinduism, Buddhism, Catholicism and Protestantism. Here are some examples to demonstrate this fact and to further explain the Scientology principles.

1. **Each person (theta) is a part or unit of the universe.**

    This scientology belief is similar to the Buddhist belief that all things in the universe are connected to one another. Each person has the goal to become an Operating Thetan (OT), who has passed all the levels of auditing and has become "clear". In this state, the person has realized his immortality as a spiritual entity.

2. **The spirit is immortal and lives on forever.**

    Scientologists believe that the spirit lives on and just transfers to a new body to be reborn. This is called reincarnation in Hinduism. Hinduism is one of the oldest religions of the same belief that the soul lives on until one reaches perfection. For Scientologists that is Theta, and for Hinduism, Buddhism and Jainism that is Nirvana or Moksha.

3. How a person lived his past life can influence his current life.

Scientologists believe that what happened in the past usually affects the present life of a person. Hence, he reaps what he sows. This is called Karma in Hinduism. It also stresses the belief that you can never run away from your past deeds. You always get what you give to others. According to Hinduism, Karma is a natural law of nature that never fails.

4. A scientologist has to come to his own understanding of God.

Scientologists are allowed to have their own interpretation of what God means to them. Other religions have a clearer concept of what their God is. On the other hand, Scientologists emphasize the god-like qualities in each individual. Although Christianity believes that there's one true God, it still advocates that each human person comes in the likeness and image of God, and that he should be seen as God by other members of the church. This is where the Christian quotation, "What you do to your brethren, you have done it to me" stems from.

5. **Man is basically good.**

   While the Catholics believe that man is born with original sin and that faith in God can save them, Scientologists believe that man is basically good and that he alone is responsible for his own salvation. Unlike Catholics, who accept some doctrines on faith alone (i.e. Blessed Trinity), Scientologists are encouraged to have their own spiritual experiences and learn from them.

   This is also the reason why Scientologists don't believe in Jesus Christ. To them, a Savior is not needed as their spirits don't need saving. They have been born already good and not sinful.

6. **Scientologists search for the meaning of their own lives**

   Spiritual meaning is discovered by the individual himself and is not forced upon him. Through his own journey, the individual learns how to advance his spiritual connection with the power. This means that man can connect to God directly without going through channels. This is one belief of the Protestants that separated them from other Christians. They believe that confessions and prayers must be directed to God alone and not to a priest. Scientologists, likewise, don't believe in confessions, but in forging their spiritual connections directly to God.

7. **In Scientology, God is the "Supreme Being"**

   This belief coincides with almost all religions that a God exists, who is a "Supreme Being"—omniscient and all powerful. Scientology, however, allows its members to seek their own connection with that "Supreme Being."

8. **Scientologists believe that "God helps those who help themselves"**

   This is a common belief in almost all religions. There are certain religions however, who stick to the edict that nothing happens without God's permission. Christians believe in this edict, but the value of hard work is also considered. This is why they value the meaning in the quote: "Man proposes, God disposes." That means that a person must try his best to work hard on his ambitions, but ultimately, it's God who will grant him success.

9. **Scientology believes that the universe is created through the theta (spirit or life force) that gives birth to the physical world of MEST (Matter, Energy, Space and Time)**

   Most religions believe in God creating the universe and everything around it. For Christians, the Bible revealed this in the Book of Genesis.

Like Scientologists, the Buddhists don't believe that God created the world either. They adhere to the belief that there are many spiritual beings and that science has the best explanation for the creation of the world.

10. Auditors eventually become ministers

This is similar to priesthood of the Catholic Church in which seminarians (auditors) are eventually ordained to priesthood once their knowledge of theology is sufficient, and their training as church leaders has been completed successfully.

What makes Scientology distinct is its focus on the person's growth and development in relation to himself, the world and the universe. It is in the belief that one can cleanse the self of past mistakes that allows its followers to attain the highest level of spiritual fulfillment.

Chapter 5: The Ceremonies of Scientology

Like any other church, there are Scientology ceremonies performed by its members. They also have ministers, which are the equivalent of priests, pastors or rabbis. However, the Scientology church is unlike other churches because of its "modern" displays such as videos, practical courses, and many other forms of communication. Other non-Scientologists call it a spiritual college, where people learn through their own and not from someone who "preaches" to them.

These are the customary Scientology ceremonies:

1. **Sunday Religious Services**

   This is the day that Scientologists enjoy a religious service according to their needs. They come together as one in communal worship. The officiating minister reads everything from a pre-prepared script based on L. Ron Hubbard's teachings, and does not conduct it extemporaneously.

   The activities include the following:

   - Reading of the Creed of Scientology

- Sermon (from L. Ron Hubbard's book)
- Scientology process
- Prayer (Prayer for Total Freedom)

2. Weddings

This is considered a momentous occasion for Scientologists in which family members and significant friends come together as one. They are present because they have to grant their agreement to the union between two individuals, who want to commit to each other.

The wedding ceremony is similar to that of other religions with the bridal procession, traditional vows, the presence of best man and maid of honor, and with the parents joining in the celebration of the meaningful union. The union of couples is part of the dynamic system that Scientologists observe. They believe that marriage, sex, procreation and raising children are essential parts of self-discovery and of the "Eight Dynamics of Existence".

During the union, the importance of implementing Scientology's ARC is stressed to the couple. ARC stands for A – Affinity, R – Reality and C – Communication.

A—The couple has to develop affinity to each other—meaning they have to continue to work on their emotional bond and love each other.

R—Reality indicates that the couple has to perceive what is real and what is not, to better understand each other.

C—Communication is the result of the first two. A healthy affinity and sense of reality leads to better communication between the couple.

3. Recognition and Namings

Namings are baptisms in Scientology. The presence of the parents and a godmother and godfather are required. The ceremony is similar to other churches, in the sense that the parents and godparents are reminded of their obligations to the child. Also, the child receives a new identity and is introduced to the congregation as a new member. The child is warmly welcomed by the members of the church.

4. Funerals

These are conducted much the same way as other churches, where parting words are given by family members and friends. Nevertheless, the ceremony is for rejoicing in the ending of an old chapter and the beginning of a new chapter for the deceased. This is due to the fact that Scientologists believe that the body is just a vessel occupied by the immortal soul. They believe that the spirit lives on and will occupy another material body to begin a new life.

5. Friday Night Graduations

As the name implies, this is done on Fridays. It's the time when those who have finally completed their auditing and training for the week are acknowledged by the congregation. This intends to motivate aspiring auditors to do their best.

The major ceremonies are typically conducted by the minister and observed by Scientologists. If you noticed, the Scientology Church operates the same way as other religions. The church is where the congregation gathers to conduct religious worships, meetings, trainings and other related activities.

Chapter 6: Controversies Involving Scientology

During the course of its existence, the Church of Scientology has undergone numerous attacks from organizations, religions, and individual entities. The church itself has created some issues towards persons and groups. Here are some of them:

1. **Copyright issues**

    There were several instances in which entities or individuals were sued by the Church of Scientology because of alleged copyright issues involving texts, symbols and similar materials belonging to Scientology. Persons who use Scientology copyrighted material without being a member were also reportedly sued.

2. **"Fair Game" policy**

    This is a policy where attackers of the Church of Scientology are subjected to the "Fair Game" policy. Reportedly, this policy was created by L. Ron Hubbard to counter attackers. The policy is said to contain instructions on how to treat attackers with an attack in return. This policy has since been declared non-existent by Scientologists, claiming that the practice has ceased already.

3. Defense in the name of religion (Operation Snow White)

L. Ron Hubbard's wife, Mary Sue Hubbard, has been reportedly convicted of domestic espionage. She had claimed freedom of religion in her defense. There are also cases of high-ranking Scientologists who were involved in criminal accusations, some of them involving questionable actions against critics of the church. Their defense was also religion.

4. The question of whether Scientology is a religion or not

Some countries, while they don't prohibit Scientology, don't recognize Scientology as a religion, and so they have not granted the church tax exemption as a religious organization in these countries. The following countries are among those that allow Scientology but have not granted tax exemption:

- Canada
- France
- Finland
- Ireland
- Germany

- United Kingdom

The Church of Scientology claimed that the controversies were created by entities, who are trying to destroy the credibility of Scientology and its members. Whether the controversies deserve a second look or should be taken nonchalantly will depend upon you as the reader.

Chapter 7: Important Pointers on Scientology

Scientology encompasses a complex area of knowledge that can be difficult to understand. Here is a condensed list of pointers that gives a general overview of Scientology:

1. **Scientology is a religion.** Scientologists make it clear that it is not a cult, but rather, an established religion. They worship and attend religious ceremonies in church like any other congregation.

2. **Scientologists welcome all.** Anyone who wishes to visit their church may do so without discrimination. You can walk-in anytime and observe their activities should you want to. There are testing, training, behavior betterment programs and religious services. The Church also welcomes inquiries and there are staff happy to give more information.

3. **Scientologists are committed to extend community services**. This is done through the Scientologists' assistance on education and support for a lot of issues such as human rights, human reforms and other worthwhile endeavors.

4. **Scientologists are advised to be optimistic.** They view life as an arena where everyone should win, and that they should be active participants in this quest. But be advised, critics are regarded with a wary eye.

5. **Achieving a "State of Clear" is a major objective in Scientology.** This is the state when a person no longer has a "reactive mind". The reactive mind is perceived as the source of irrational and unwanted behaviors. Hence, when a person is clear, he responds calmly and rationally to other people's actions.

6. **Scientology involves a technology that has been reportedly tested by L. Ron Hubbard.** All these are contained in his writings, which Scientologists adapted as their way of life.

7. **Auditing and training are essential parts of Scientology.** A member can never become a great Scientologist if he doesn't participate in auditing and training. These are all parts of the member's development and spiritual growth.

8. **Scientology is not taught or lectured on.** The presence of the Course Supervisor during training is to help direct students to L. Ron Hubbard's organized study materials. The Course Supervisor is not allowed to interpret but should only act as a guide. The

student is directly connected to the Scientology material himself.

9. **Study Technology is the best method used to study Scientology**. It's a method that Hubbard created to help students understand easily the concepts of Scientology. But the method, known also as Study Tech, can be used for other courses, as well.

10. **Scientology has a worldwide following consisting of non-profit and for-profit organizations.** There are no exact numbers of the members of Scientology, but reports approximate around 40,000 to 50,000 members. There were reports of a slow decline in the numbers, but nothing has been confirmed due to conflicting reports.

11. **Donations for the church are encouraged in Scientology.** Just like other churches, the congregation is encouraged to donate for social betterment activities, church and congregation expansion, and ministers' training.

12. **The Sea Organization in Scientology is equivalent to an order in the Catholic Church.** The Sea Organization is composed of dedicated members who undergo training so that they could

dedicate their whole life in the service of Scientology. This is what they call the "vow of service".

13. **The Scientology Church does not endorse psychiatric treatment.** This is because Scientologists believe that psychiatric treatment can be inhumane at times. They also believe that only the spirit can properly heal the body.

14. **Scientology is an "action" religion and not a "belief" religion.** For one to become a genuine Scientologist, he must act out the teachings, and not just believe in them. This is the only way that he can answer his own spiritual questions and develop himself towards being an OT.

15. **Scientologists believe that their philosophies are based on scientific processes.** Although some scientists reportedly disagree with the Scientology's interpretation of science, Scientologists hold firm that their beliefs are scientifically sound.

L. Ron Hubbard has written a number of books on what Scientology is grounded on. The following books will prove useful in deepening your understanding of this belief system:

- **A History of Man**
- **Dianetics: The Modern Science of Mental Health**
- **The Scientology Handbook**
- **Science of Survival**
- **Scientology 0-8**

All of these books are used during auditing and training and you can access these books from Scientology churches when you go visiting. There are also videos and tests that you can opt to avail of, should you want to go on an in-depth study of Scientology.

Conclusion

Everyone is welcome in the Church of Scientology. The fact remains that in spite of all the controversies, Scientology has reportedly brought enlightenment and wisdom to its "visitors" or "walk-ins". As one visitor aptly stated, after walking into one of the Scientology Churches, "It's like a spiritual college."

However, the spiritual journey of each individual depends upon himself—alone. Scientologists believe that you can never force anyone to believe in something he does not have conviction for. Therefore, Scientology is a personal journey that you have to undertake towards a more meaningful existence with the aid of auditors and trainers. Take note, they're only there to listen (auditors) and to guide you (trainers).

You can arrive at your own conclusions based on the information presented here. Whether it's a positive or negative conclusion, will be all up to you. I worked to ensure that there are no biases in the presentation of what Scientology is all about in this book, so it is presumed that you can conclude correctly.

And so now the big question: Is Scientology worth your time? Do you want to practice the principles of Scientologists? If you have firm conviction in its beliefs and would like to consider becoming a member of the Church of Scientology, schedule a visit and meet with practitioners. This is the only way you can learn how to fully practice its principles. Decide wisely. Remember, that once you join the church, it must be for good. In addition, you will have to become an active member, and follow the rules set by the congregation. Good luck!

Finally, I'd like to thank you for purchasing this book! If you found it helpful, I'd greatly appreciate it if you'd take a moment to leave a review on Amazon. Thank you!

Printed in Great Britain
by Amazon